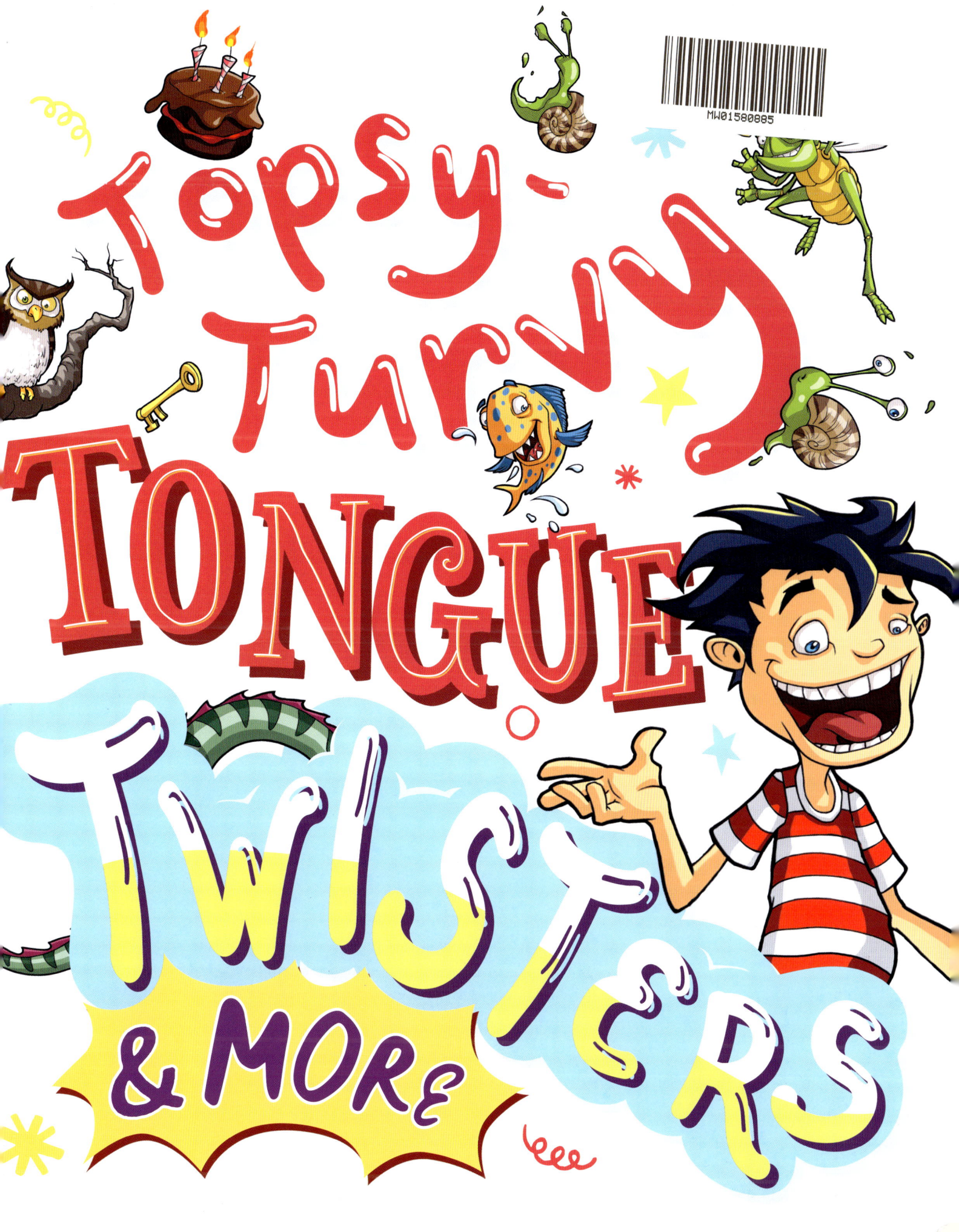

Silver Dolphin Books
An imprint of Printers Row Publishing Group
A division of Readerlink Distribution Services, LLC.
10350 Barnes Canyon Road, Suite 100, San Diego, CA 92121
www.silverdolphinbooks.com

Copyright © 2019 Hinkler Books Pty Ltd

All rights reserved. No part of this publication may be reproduced, distributed, or transmitted in any form or by any means, including photocopying, recording, or other electronic or mechanical methods, without the prior written permission of the publisher, except in the case of brief quotations embodied in critical reviews and certain other noncommercial uses permitted by copyright law.

Printers Row Publishing Group is a division of Readerlink Distribution Services, LLC.
Silver Dolphin Books is a registered trademark of Readerlink Distribution Services, LLC.

All notations of errors or omissions should be addressed to Silver Dolphin Books, Editorial Department, at the above address. All other correspondence (author inquiries, permissions) concerning the content of this book should be addressed to:

Hinkler Books Pty Ltd
45-55 Fairchild Street
Heatherton Victoria 3202 Australia
www.hinkler.com
Illustrated by Glen Singleton
Writing and compiling by Katie Hewat
Cover design by Hinkler Studio
Typesetting by MPS Limited

ISBN: 978-1-68412-594-4
Manufactured, printed, and assembled in Heshan, Guangdong, China.
First printing, February 2019. LP/02/19
23 22 21 20 19   1 2 3 4 5

Contents

Absurd Animals	4
Gross Gags	26
Game On!	37
The Five Senses	49
Crazy Critters and Cool Characters	60
Perfectly Prehistoric	82
Tough and Tricky	93
Letters and Numbers	122
Water Works	141
Strange School and Wacky Work	152
Freaky Food	167
Silly Stuff	179

Absurd Animals

Riddles

What do well-behaved young lambs say to their mothers?

"Thank-ewe."

Why did the crowd faint when the parrot started talking?

It had fowl breath!

What do elephants play marbles with?

Bowling balls.

What asks but never answers?

An owl.

What has six legs and can fly long distances?

Three swallows.

What's black and white and eats like a horse?

A zebra.

What's the same size and shape as an elephant but weighs nothing at all?

An elephant's shadow.

When is a car like a frog?

When it is being toad.

How do you spell "mousetrap" with only three letters?

C-A-T.

Absurd Animals

Absurd Animals

What did the buffalo say to his son, when he went away on a long trip?

"Bison."

If a horse loses its tail, where can it get another one?

At a re-tail store.

How do you know when it's been raining cats and dogs?

You step in a poodle.

How many animals did Moses fit in the Ark?

None, it was Noah's Ark.

How do you get down from an elephant?

You don't get down from an elephant; you get down from a duck.

What's bright orange and sounds like a parrot?

A carrot.

What does an octopus wear when it's cold?

A coat of arms.

LAUNDRY DAY AT THE OCTOPUS'S HOUSE

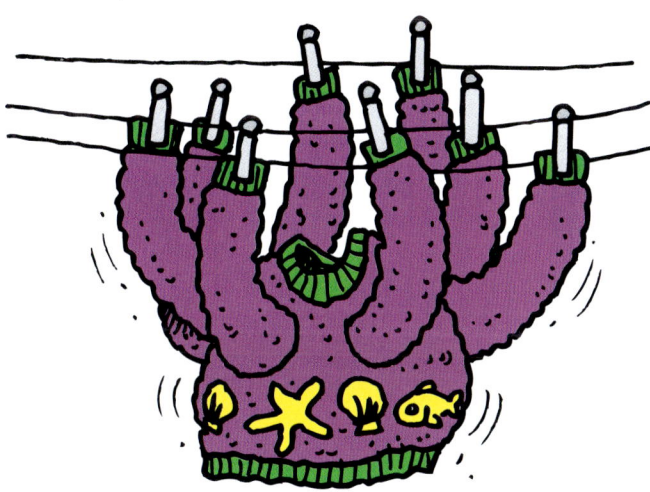

What's the difference between a dark sky and an injured lion?

One pours with rain and the other roars with pain.

What would you get if you crossed a hunting dog with a journalist?

A newshound.

What happened to the two frogs that caught the same bug at the same time?

They were tongue-tied.

Absurd Animals

7

Absurd Animals

Why do camels love Wednesday so much?

It's hump day!

Why are fish clever?

Because they live in schools.

What do bees do with their honey?

They cell it.

What do you call a cat who lives in a hospital?

A first-aid kitty.

What do you call a cowboy cat?

Puss in boots.

What can go as fast as a racehorse?

The jockey.

Why is the letter "t" important to a stick insect?

Because without it, it would be a sick insect.

Why should you be careful playing against a team of big cats?

They might be cheetahs.

I'm the part of a bird that's not in the sky; I can swim in the ocean and remain dry. What am I?

Its shadow.

What's a shark's favorite candy?

Jawbreakers!

What's the difference between a bird and a fly?

A bird can fly but a fly can't bird.

Absurd Animals

What is more fantastic than a talking dog?

A spelling bee.

When is a brown dog not a brown dog?

When it's a greyhound.

What do you call a bee that is always complaining?

A grumble bee.

How do you stop a dog from digging up the front yard?

Put it out in the backyard.

Why does a tiger have stripes?

So it won't be spotted.

What is a prickly pear?

Two hedgehogs.

How can you tell a dogwood tree?

By its bark.

What do you get if you cross a worm with a baby goat?

A dirty kid.

What kind of sharks never eat women?

Man-eating sharks!

What has four legs and an arm?

A hungry lion.

Why was the glowworm unhappy?

Her children weren't very bright.

Absurd Animals

Absurd Animals

When is it bad luck to be followed by a big black cat?

When you are a little gray mouse.

Why are giraffes good friends to have?

Because they stick their necks out for you.

Why was the mother flea so sad?

Because her children were going to the dogs.

Where do you find a no-legged dog?

Right where you left it.

What's green and red and goes 120 mph?

A frog in a blender.

What fly has laryngitis?

A hoarsefly

What's black and white and rolls down a hill?

A penguin.

What's black and white and laughs?

The penguin that pushed the other one down the hill.

What happened to the horse that swallowed a dollar?

He bucked.

What animal builds his house in the jungle?

A boa constructor.

Absurd Animals

Absurd Animals

What has 50 legs and can't walk?
Half a centipede.

What do you get when an elephant stands on your roof?
Mushed rooms.

What did the alien sheep say when they landed?
"We come in fleece!"

What do polar bears get from sitting on the ice too long?
Polaroids.

Why do gorillas have big nostrils?
Because they have big fingers.

What's an army of worms called?

An apple corps.

What's the last thing that goes through a bug's mind as it hits a car windscreen?

His bottom.

What do you get when you cross a rooster with a steer?

A cock-and-bull story.

What's worse than finding a worm in your apple?

Finding half a worm!

Why didn't the bird study for the test?

She decided to wing it!

Absurd Animals

A hundred feet in the air and yet my back is still on the ground. What am I?

An upside-down centipede.

What do you get if you sit under a cow?

A pat on the head.

Where did Noah keep the bees?

In the Ark hives.

Which bird can lift the most?

A crane.

What college degree did the baboon get?

Monkey Business Administration!

What has a foot but no legs?

A snail.

What has four legs and flies?

A smelly cat.

What do you call a lion wearing a hat?

A dandy lion.

What is gray, has a tail and a trunk but is not an elephant?

A mouse on vacation.

What do you call a lamb with a machine gun?

Lambo.

Why are naughty kids like maggots?

Because they try to wiggle out of everything.

What do you get when you cross a vehicle with a dog?

A carpet.

Absurd Animals

When do you put a frog in your sister's bed?

When you can't find a mouse.

What did the frog say when he was asked to the prom?

Toad-ally!

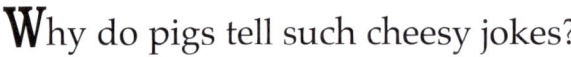

Why do pigs tell such cheesy jokes?

They're hams!

Why don't turkeys get invited to dinner parties?

Because they use fowl language.

If a rooster laid a brown egg and a white egg, what color would the chicks be?

Roosters don't lay eggs.

Why wasn't the butterfly invited to the dance?

Because it was a moth ball.

If a man carried my burden, he'd break his back. I am not rich, but I always leave silver in my trail. What am I?

A snail.

What part of a fish weighs the most?

The scales.

Why do elephants have trunks?

Because they can't fit everything in their purses.

What do you say when you meet a toad?

"Wart's new?"

Absurd Animals

Where do you find elephants?

You don't. They're so big they don't get lost.

What language do birds speak?

Pigeon Latin.

Why do crows like shiny things?

Because diamonds are a bird's best friend!

What do you have when twenty rabbits step backward?

A receding hare-line.

You are in a room with a lemur, a chimpanzee and a gorilla. Which primate in the room is smartest?

You are!

What do you call an amorous insect?

A love bug.

A monkey, a squirrel, and a bird race to the top of a coconut tree. Who reaches the banana first?

None of them. There are no bananas is coconut trees.

Why do chickens lay eggs?

Because if they drop them they will break.

What walks on its head all day?

A nail in a horseshoe.

Where do fish keep their money?

In a river bank.

Who always goes to sleep wearing shoes?

A horse.

Absurd Animals

What time is it when an elephant sits on your fence?

Time to get a new fence.

What's big, has antlers, and is easily frightened?

A scaredy-moose!

I have a little house in which I live in all alone. It has no doors or windows, and if I want to go out I must break through the wall. What am I?

A baby bird in an egg.

What is the single greatest use of cowhide?

Covering cows.

Who kidnapped the princess fly?

The dragonfly!

Tongue Twisters

The thick, slippery snake sneaked and slithered.

The fleeing fly finally flew fast.

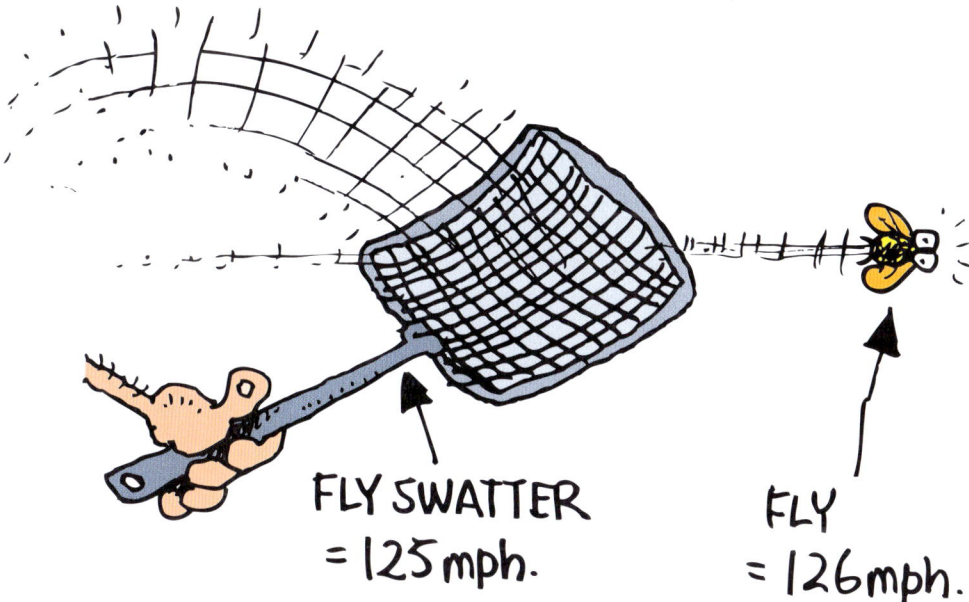

FLY SWATTER = 125 mph.

FLY = 126 mph.

Four frozen flies were free to flee.

The tired turtle tried to tread tenderly.

The sleek, shiny shark swam silently.

Those sleek shiny sharks sure do swim silently!

The dreary donkey drank delicately.

Ordinarily, orange orangutans organized orderly outings.

Polly parrot plucked perfectly plump peppers.

The porpoise purposely performed profound poetry.

The offbeat octopus awkwardly awoke.

Pigeons sure sit shyly on statues.

The dog dragged Daisy's dolly for digging.

The stinger stung Sheryl with a sharp stab.

Paulie Bull pulled but Billy Pug bailed.

When Warren Rabbit really wanted he'd rush into his rabbit warren.

Absurd Animals

GROSS GAGS

Riddles

What's invisible and smells like carrots?

Bunny farts.

What do you call an elephant that never washes?

A smellyphant.

What's yellow and smells like bananas?

Monkey vomit.

How can you tell when a moth farts?
It flies straight for a second.

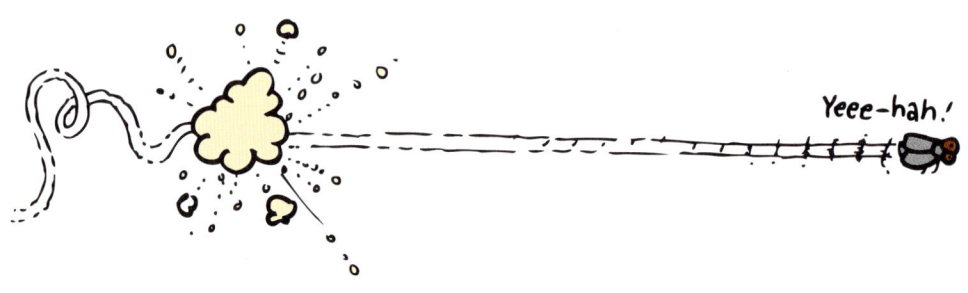

What's brown and sounds like a bell?

Dung.

What do you give an elephant with diarrhea?

Plenty of room.

What do you give a nauseous elephant?

A very big paper bag.

When Nancy said she had a rumble in her tummy... everyone knew just what she meant!

What's a sick joke?

Something that comes up in conversation.

What's the hardest part about sky diving?

The ground.

How do you make a Venetian blind?

Poke his eyes out.

How can you tell if a corpse is angry?

It flips its lid.

Gross Gags

What do you find up a clean nose?

Fingerprints.

Why didn't the man die when he drank poison?

Because he was in the living room.

What's green, has two legs and sits on the end of your finger?

The boogeyman.

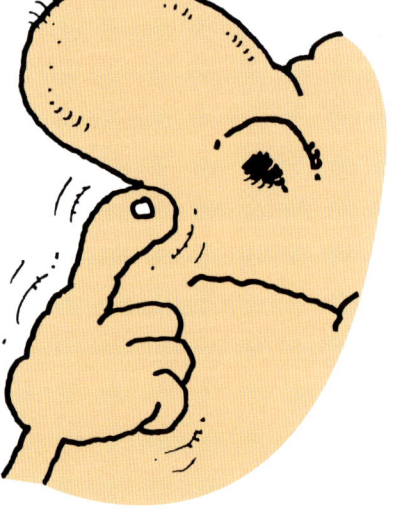

What do you do if your nose goes on strike?

Picket!

What did the smelly man use to perfume his bathroom?

Poo-pourri!

How did the basketball get wet?

The players dribbled all over it.

How do you make a tissue dance?

Put some boogie into it.

What is the difference between broccoli and boogers?

Kids don't like to eat broccoli.

What did one toilet say to the other toilet?

"You look a little flushed!"

What did the first mate see in the toilet?

The captain's log.

What do you call someone who's run out of things to do in the ocean?

Surf-bored!

Gross Gags

What happens when the queen burps?

She issues a royal pardon.

Why didn't the girl forgive her friend for picking his nose?

It was **SNOT** okay!

Why did the boy take his own toilet paper to the party?

Because he was a party pooper.

Why do they have fences around graveyards?

Everyone is dying to get in.

What's green and slimy and hangs from trees?

Giraffe boogers.

Why did the toilet paper roll down the hill?

To get to the bottom.

What's another name for a snail?

A booger with a crash helmet.

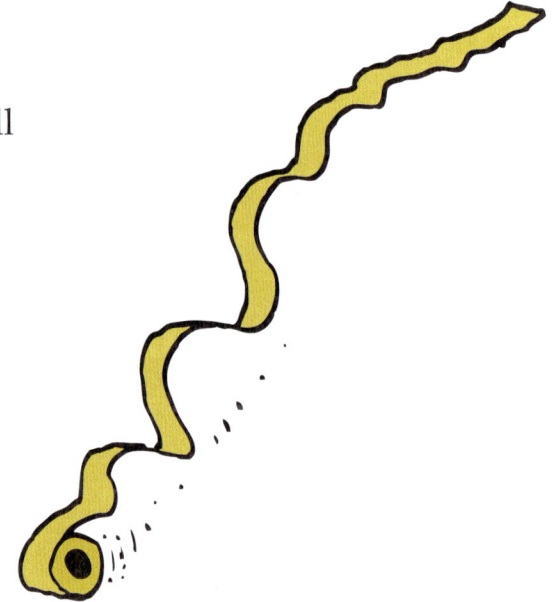

What do you do with crude oil?

Teach it some manners.

How do you keep flies out of the kitchen?

Put a pile of manure in the living room.

What's the difference between a maggot and a cockroach?

Cockroaches crunch more when you eat them.

What tastes worse than eating slugs?

Throwing them back up again!

What has two gray legs and two brown legs?

An elephant with diarrhea.

What's red, brown and hairy?

Jelly toast, dropped on carpet.

Tongue Twisters

A vampire thirstily sucked thick blood.
He glugged, gobbled, gargled and gulped.
He swished, swirled and swallowed.

Seven short, slimy zombies sloshed, slipped, and slid on a shiny, slippery slide.

Four fighting flatulent fighters farted frequently while fighting ferociously.

Can you can a can as a canner can can a can?

Which wristwatches are Swiss wristwatches?

The queen quite cleverly created chaos with a steamy stinker.

Thick, slimy sticky snot.

Gooey poo on Stewie's shoe.

Brock's BO brought Bob to tears.

Doreen's double Dutch oven disgusted Darren.

Really waxy ears are ringing.

He threw three free throws!

Seth's stomach solemnly sent puke spewing.

My smelly, slimy, stinky sister's sloppy diapers.

Sweat-soaked smelly armpit stink.

A skunk sat on a stump and thought the stump stunk, but the stump thought the skunk stunk!

Frank's farts freaked Francine.

Sammy's sweaty shirt was soaked in sweat.
Silly Sally slipped on Sammy's sloppy sweat.
Simple Simon swam in Sammy's sweat.
Sammy simply said, *"That's wet."*

The blob was a blobby gooey glob.

Tongue twisters twist tongues. Twisted tongues taste terrible. Terrible tasting tongues twist tightly. A toast to tightly twisted terrible-tasting tongues.

Suddenly, Samuel saw snotty Sarah stealing several strands of snot.

Bob's big burp blasted barriers.

Paul popped his pus-filled pimple.

Betty bet Poppy that basketball players have BO problems.

Girl gargoyle, guy gargoyle, gurgling gluey goo.

Gross Gags

Eric's earwax was orange, obviously.

Gertie gurgled good blood and bad blood.

Flora's flatulence floored frightened Freddy.

If Fey farted, Fiona fell, and Frannie fainted, how foul was Flora's fart?

Chucky's upchuck had colorful carrot chunks.

Octavia's obscene old upchuck was oddly orange.

Six snot balls shot past Sally Schnell.

Game On!

Riddles

What is put on the table and cut, but never eaten.

A deck of cards.

What does every winner lose in a race?

Their breath.

What stories are told by basketball players?

Tall tales.

Why did all the bowling pins go down?

They were on strike.

What has 22 legs and two wings but cannot fly?

A soccer team.

Which goalkeeper can jump higher than the goal posts?

All of them—goal posts can't jump!

Why did the soccer player take a piece of rope onto the field?

He was the skipper.

What part of a football ground smells the best?

Scenter field.

When are babies like basketball players?

When they dribble.

What illness do martial artists get?

Kung flu.

Why were the arrows nervous?

Because they were all in a quiver.

Who was the fastest runner in the whole world?

Adam, because he was the first in the human race.

What do you call a puppy who delivers presents?

Santa Paws!

What did one bowling ball say to the other?

"Don't stop me, I'm on a roll!"

What's the best way to win a race?

Run faster than everyone else.

Where do old bowling balls end up?

In the gutter.

What was the fly doing in the lady's soup?

The Backstroke.

What falls in winter but never gets hurt?

Snow!

Why don't grasshoppers go to football games?

They prefer cricket.

What did the smelly runner say before the race?

"Ready, Sweat, Go!"

Why aren't football stadiums built in outer space?

Because there is no atmosphere!

Why is tennis such a noisy game?

Because everyone raises a racket.

Why did the bicycle keep falling over?

Because it was two tired.

When is it handy to have toes?

When you go to a foot ball.

What is harder to catch the faster you run?

Your breath.

Tongue Twisters

Wayne likes white-water rafting after work.

Bree's billiards brilliance bewildered Brooke.

A broad boy boxed blindly.

Trevor's trophy for the table-tennis triumph was terrific.

Boris beat Barney in breaststroke.

Willie's really weary.

Sprinting Sally shot over hurdles.

One-one was a race horse. Two-two was one too. One-one won one race. Two-two won one too.

The athletes decided to discuss discus delegations.

Shot-puts squash feet.

Callum's karate class created classic karate kicks.

The fighters frightened fans fighting a frighteningly fearsome fight.

The wild, wide wrestler went wacko.

The quick quiet cricketer requested cricket competitors.

Stanley loved sitting, sipping soda on his sofa, seeing stunned skiers stacking in snow. Seriously, Stanley loved seeing sporting slip-ups.

Prince Paul played polo pretty poorly.

Wrestlers wearing lycra are really weird.

The good golfer's green golf glove.

Relay runners run relays really regularly.

Paul played plinky, plonky ping-pong.

Barbara's barbed-wire barbell.

Floundering Freya felt the burn.

Darren dropped a dumbbell on his dad.

Sandy skipped swiftly.

Biceps, triceps, thigh sets, high reps.

Sandy surely showed super cycling style.

Tim took training tips and the training tips Tim took taught Tim to train.

Tony tried Terry's treadmill.

The golfer gripped the golf grip grudgingly.

Sarah's sixth cycling session surely sucked.

Bobby the baseballer briefly broke baseball bats by bashing baseballs.

Push-ups, press-ups, pull-ups, sit-ups.

Peggy Babcock puffed and panted in pilates class.

We surely shall see the sun shine soon.

Brad's bulging biceps burst.

Stewart slipped and tripped on the steep slope he trekked.

All it took to start an avalanche was for Stewart to slip and trip...

Brandon's black boxing gloves broke bashing punching bags.

The Five Senses

Riddles

What can you hear but not see and only speaks when it is spoken to?

An echo.

What has eyes that cannot see, a tongue that cannot taste and a soul that cannot die?

A shoe.

What is there more of the less you see?

Darkness.

What can you hold without touching?

Your breath.

Why did the Invisible Man's wife understand him so well?
Because she could see right through him.

What can you hold but never touch?
A conversation.

What kind of music do fathers like to sing?
Pop music.

What did the parents say to their son who wanted to play drums?
"Beat it!"

What did one ear say to the other ear?
"Between you and me, we need a haircut."

What can be caught but never seen?
A remark.

What did the ear 'ear?

Only the nose knows.

What tastes better than it smells?

A tongue.

You can touch me, but not see me. You can throw me out, but not away. What am I?

Your back.

Why should you never tell secrets in a grocery store?

Because the corn has ears, potatoes have eyes, and beanstalk.

Why do farts smell?

So that deaf people can appreciate them too.

What did the floor say to the desk?

I can see your drawers.

The Five Senses

The Five Senses

What do you think when you see a monster?

I hope he hasn't seen me.

The person who makes it doesn't need it, the person who buys it doesn't use it, and the person who uses it can't see or hear it. What is it?

A coffin.

What kind of music do zombies like best?

Soul.

What did the digital clock say to its mother?

Look Mom, no hands!

What smells funny?

Clown poo.

Why do robots hear so well?

They're all gears!

What has eyes but cannot see?

A potato.

Say my name and I disappear. What am I?

Silence.

What do you call a color-blind dog?

A greyhound!

The Five Senses

Tongue Twisters

Fergus felt furry fungus.

Larry liked licking yellow lollipops.

High notes, low notes, fast notes, slow notes, loud notes, soft notes, big nose, no nose.

Trevor's triangle tinkled and tingled.

Seth's breath smelled like death.

Which wise guy's eyes spied the high-priced prize?

The selfish elf ate shellfish.

Ten top-notch cops felt fob watch knobs.

The deer's ears clearly hear another deer's fairly near.

Freddy's feet smelled foul.

The brilliant big brass band played beautifully.

Sheila said she smelled Schmidt shaving.

Terry tastes twelve turnips, turning Terry's tongue numb.

Yola loves yummy gumbo.

Simon sang several sweet-sounding songs.

A small, steamy smell silently slipped out.

Chase chews cud. Cows chew cud. If cows chase Chase, is a Chase a cud-chewing cow?

The crazy composer caused chaos, creating cringe-worthy compositions.

Can the toucan touch two tin cans?

Morose music makes Margaret mournful.

Kim counted colors she could see on Kevin's couch.

Brad's bassoon broke, bruising Brad badly.

The drummer dumbly decided to drum at dawn.

Horace hid when he heard Herod honking.

Violent violinist.

The string section suddenly went on strike, sending shockwaves shooting through the symphony.

After the opera, Owen often opted for orange juice.

Stacey baked stinky scones.

Muriel miraculously made magical music.
Muriel's miraculously magical music was marvelous.

Trevor terribly trumpeted till Trixie trampled Trevor's trumpet.

Crazy Critters and Cool Characters

Riddles

What would you call Superman if he lost all his powers?

Man.

What did one angel say to the other angel?

"Halo."

Who's afraid of wolves and has a potty mouth?

Little Rude Riding Hood.

Where do you find giant snails?
At the ends of their fingers.

How did the Vikings send messages?
By Norse code.

What is big, red, and eats rocks?
A big, red rock eater.

Which of the witch's friends eats the fastest?
The goblin.

Why was the fish dressed up like the Pope?
He was a holy mackerel!

What is Dracula's favorite fruit?

Necktarines.

What do Alexander the Great and Kermit the Frog have in common?

They have the same middle name!

Why was Thomas Edison able to invent the light bulb?

Because he was very bright.

Why did Dracula take medicine?

To stop his coffin.

Why did the vampire go to the orthodontist?

To improve his bite.

What's the difference between Santa Claus and a warm dog?

Santa wears the suit, but the dog just pants.

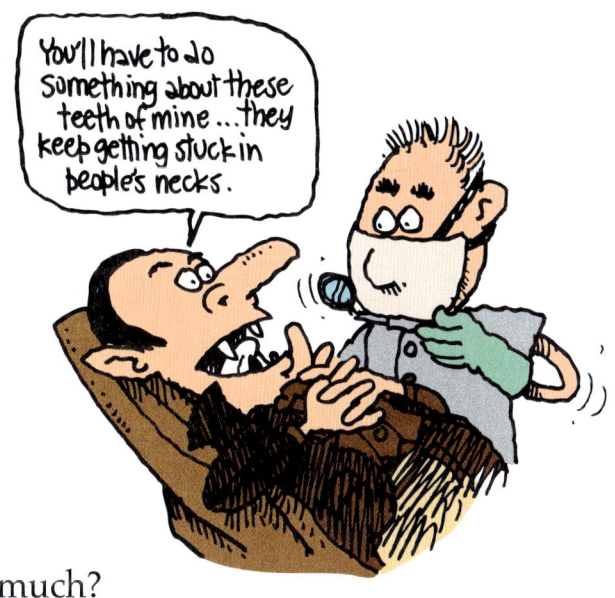

Why do trains love food so much?

They love to chew-chew!

Who steals from her Grandma's house?

Little Red Robbing Hood.

Why is the vampire so unpopular?

Because he is a pain in the neck.

What kind of cheese do monsters eat?

Monsterella!

During which battle was Lord Nelson killed?

His last one.

What did Cinderella say when her photos didn't arrive?

"Some day my prints will come."

Who delivers Christmas presents to the wrong houses?

Santa Flaws.

What do monsters have mid-morning?

A coffin break.

What did Santa Claus's wife say during the thunderstorm?

"Come and look at the rain, dear."

What job does Dracula have with the Transylvanian baseball team?

He's the bat boy.

Who was the father of the Black Prince?

Old King Coal.

How did Noah steer the Ark at night?

He switched on the floodlights.

Why did the young vampire follow his dad's profession?

Because it was in his blood.

What's the name of a clever monster?

Frank Einstein.

Which bus could sail the oceans?

Columbus.

What did the cannibal say to the explorer?

"Nice to eat you."

What do you get if you cross a skunk with a bear?

Winnie the Pooh.

What does a monster call his parents?

Dead and Mummy.

Why do witches get good bargains?

They're good at haggling.

Why did the Cyclops give up teaching?

Because he only had one pupil.

Why don't cannibals eat comedians?

Because they taste funny.

What feature do witches love on their computers?

The spell-checker.

What do you call a witch that lives at the beach?

A sand witch!

What does a ghost read every day?

His horrorscope.

What did King Kong say when his sister had a baby?

"Well, I'll be a monkey's uncle!"

Where does Dracula wash?

In a bloodbath.

What do vampires cross the sea in?

Blood vessels.

Why did the zombie decide to stay in his coffin?

He felt rotten.

When do ghosts usually appear?

Just before someone screams.

Where does Dracula go fishing?

In a bloodstream.

What did the witch say to the vampire?

"Get a life!"

What do you get when you cross a computer with a vampire?

Love at first byte.

How do monsters like their eggs?

Terrifried.

Snow White and the Seven Dwarfs were having dinner. The dwarfs asked for more food so Snow White got them some. How many seconds did she take?

Seven.

What does a monster eat after he's been to the dentist?

The dentist.

What do sea monsters eat?

Fish and ships.

What do you do with a blue monster?

Try to cheer him up.

Who is the best dancer at a monster party?

The boogie man.

What should you take if a monster invites you to dinner?

Someone who can't run as fast as you.

Why isn't the Abominable Snowman scared of people?

Because he doesn't believe in them.

What does a monster mommy say to her kids at dinnertime?

"Don't chew with someone in your mouth."

Why did the monster eat his music teacher?

Because his Bach was worse than his bite.

What's a witch's favorite subject in school?

Spelling.

On which day do monsters eat people?

Chewsday.

What do ghosts use to type letters?

A type-frighter.

Why are Cyclops couples happy together?

Because they always see eye to eye.

What does a boy monster do when a girl monster rolls her eyes at him?

He rolls them back to her.

Why do ghosts hate rain?

It dampens their spirits.

What do you call a good-looking, kind, and considerate monster?

A complete failure.

Why don't ghosts bother telling lies?

Because you can see right through them.

What do you call the winner of a monster beauty contest?

Ugly.

What type of horses do monsters ride?

Night mares.

What do you call a fairy that hasn't taken a bath?

Stinkerbell.

What weapon was most feared by medieval knights?

A can opener.

How does a yeti feel when it gets a cold?

Abominable.

What's green, sits in the corner and cries?

The Incredible Sulk.

If you crossed the Loch Ness monster with a shark, what would you get?

Loch jaws.

What did the skeleton say to the twin witches?

Which witch is which?

How many witches does it take to change a light bulb?

Just one, but she changes it into a toad.

Where do skeletons go swimming?

In the dead sea.

What game do young ghosts love?

Hide and shriek.

How can you tell what a ghost is getting for its birthday?

By feeling its presents.

What illness can you get from eating Christmas decorations?

Tinselitis.

What should you say when you meet a ghost?

"How do you boo, sir?"

What does a vampire never order at a restaurant?

Stake.

Why didn't the skeleton go to the dance?

He had no body to go with.

How do you make a skeleton laugh?

Tickle his funnybone.

Do zombies have trouble getting dates?

No, they can usually dig someone up.

Tongue Twisters

Mallory the mermaid mostly made mischief.

A pixie proudly picked a perfect present.

Mermaids mainly mingle in lagoons.

Clara cleverly created classic car tricks.

The greedy giant ground bones.

Grant the giant generally jogged gratefully.

When Grant jogged, the Earth shook.

The gabbling, gargling goblin gobbled and gargled.

The braggin', arrogant, boastin' dragon.

Bread grinding bones.

Slick Trixie, the tricky pixie, picked sticks.

A werewolf was really wary of rabies.

Michael's mighty mystical magic manipulated Maxine.

Casting and conjuring and creating confusion,
illuminating and inventing and instigating illusion.

Trudy tried teaching Tyler trickery.

Wally wished he was a wizard.
Why did Wally wish for wizardry?
Really, what Wally wanted was really wicked wizard-wear.

Which witch is which?

Five fairies flipped fifty flapjacks.

A wacky wizard with white whiskers waved his wand.

The wry wizard regularly worked on wand-waving.

The sorcerer practiced prickly imprisoning potions privately; practicing privately perfected potions perfectly.

The alien alliance allowed acrobatic eating.

The grinning gargoyle greedily gobbled green grapes.

Horrid Harriet hated Halloween.
Horrid Harriet found Halloween harrowing.
Horrid Harriet had had it with Halloween,
So Horrid Harriet headed to Hawaii.

Frankenstein found France frustrating.

Ghastly ghosts and grinning ghouls.

A werewolf's whiskers rarely waver.

Good ghosts generally greet guests jovially.

Which witch doctor rain danced?

Perfectly Prehistoric

Riddles

What do you get when a dinosaur skydives?

A big hole.

Why are old dinosaur bones kept in a museum?

Because they can't find any new ones.

What do you get when you cross a dinosaur with a vampire?

A blood shortage.

I vant to sark your blurd...

How do dinosaurs pass tests?

With extinction.

What do you get if you give a dinosaur a pogo stick?

Big holes in your driveway.

What do you call a dinosaur that destroys everything in its path?

Tyrannosaurus Wrecks.

What do you call a dinosaur that's a noisy sleeper?

Brontosnorus.

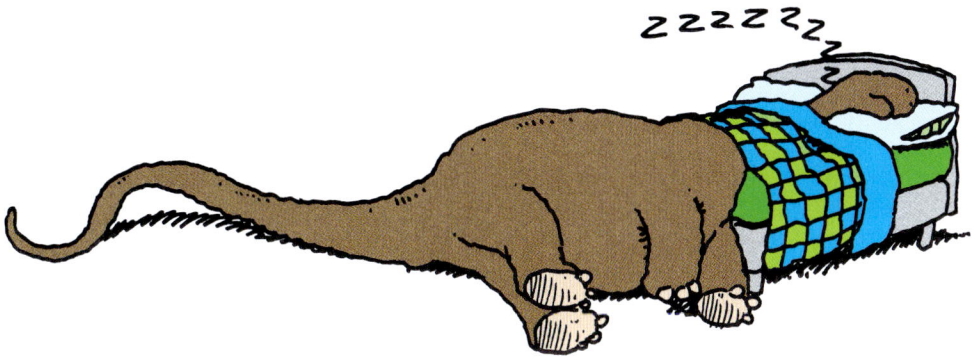

What do you call a blind dinosaur?

Do-ya-think-he-saurus.

Perfectly Prehistoric

What does a *Triceratops* sit on?

Its Tricera-bottom!

What's worse than a *Tyrannosaurus* with a toothache?

A *Diplodocus* with a sore throat.

What do you get if you cross a dinosaur with a dog?

A very nervous postal worker.

Why don't more dinosaurs join the police force?

They can't hide behind billboards.

What did the egg say to the dinosaur?

"You're egg-stinct."

Why didn't the dinosaur cross the road?

Because roads hadn't been invented yet.

Why couldn't the long-necked dinosaur see?

Because his head was in the clouds.

What do you call a group of people who dig for dinosaur bones?

A skeleton crew.

What do you call a scared *Tyrannosaurus*?

A nervous rex.

What's extinct and works in rodeos?

Broncosaurus.

Perfectly Prehistoric

What do you call a dinosaur eating a taco?

Tyrannosaurus Mex.

When did the last dinosaur die?

After the second-last dinosaur.

What do you call a 100-million-year-old dinosaur?

A fossil.

What do dinosaurs put on their floors?

Rep-tiles.

What's the hardest part of making dinosaur stew?

Finding a pot big enough to hold the dinosaur.

Why did the baby dinosaur get arrested?
Because he took the bus home.

What has a spiked tail, plates on its back, and wheels?
A *Stegosaurus* on roller skates.

Tongue Twisters

A *Brachiosaurus* bellowed with bronchitis.

Bronwyn bathed the baby *Brontosaurus* in blue bathwater.

The fabulous fabrosaurus fabricated fabulously.

Two tricky trilobites tickled Trixie.

The terribly tiring *Pterodactyl* was tragically trapped.

Saltasaurus shins should be shaved and saved.

The dopey dinosaur drank and dived and drowned.

Warren wanted a real wheel to do real wheelies;
What Warren really wanted was a real wheel.
Warren wished wheels were real,
But for cavemen wheels weren't real.

The saber-tooth slayed a sleuth.

Perfectly Prehistoric

Perfectly Prehistoric

The creepy caveman crept quite creepily.

The spiky *Stegosaurus* sipped a soda.

The tricky *Triceratops* tripped a *Tyrannosaurus*.

The brown *Brontosaurus* borrowed bright but bland books.

Manny was a whale while Sammy was a mammoth.

Naughty Neanderthals neatly gnawed a nifty numbat.

The itchy *Iguanodon* insists on eating Iggy's insects.

Fred found freaky fossils that fueled his fire for finding facts.

What do you call a dinosaur who's a karate master?

A Tricera-chops!

Sneaky sauropods eat selfish shellfish.

Shy *Styracosaurus* sometimes sheds a single shiny tear.

Perfectly Prehistoric

Vera the vivacious *Velociraptor* visits Vic with vigor.

An affable *Afrovenator* aptly ate an apple after every act.

Can *Camarasaurus* catch a crafty Camaro?

Sixty-seven thick, thoughtless, sick *Stegosauruses* stuck spikes in twenty-two trapped *Tyrannosauruses*.

Stewie the *Stegosaurus* slept soundly; Stewie the *Stegosaurus* snored solidly.

Riddles

What's easier to give than receive?

Criticism.

What kind of dress can never be worn?

Your address.

What's the last thing you take off before bed?

Your feet off the floor.

What can go up a chimney down, but not down a chimney up?

An umbrella.

Tough and Tricky

What starts working only when it's fired?

A rocket.

What is always coming but never arrives?

Tomorrow.

What stays in the corner but travels all around the world?

A postage stamp.

What do you put in a barrel to make it lighter?

A hole.

What comes down but never goes up?

Rain.

What gets wet the more you dry?

A towel.

What sort of ring is always square?

A boxing ring.

What kind of bow can't be tied?

A rainbow.

What runs all around a pasture but never moves?

A fence.

I am tall when I'm young and short when I'm old, what am I?

A candle.

What goes up and down but never moves?

A flight of stairs.

Which candle burns longer, a red one or a green one?

Neither. They both burn shorter.

What belongs to you but is used more by other people?

Your name.

What's always taken before you get it?

Your picture.

Poor people have me. Rich people need me. If you eat me you die. What am I?

Nothing.

What can you give away but also keep?

A cold.

What can run but can't walk?

A river.

Betty rode into town on Friday, and rode out again two days later, on Friday. How?

Friday was the horse's name.

If a yellow house is made of yellow bricks and a red house is made of red bricks, what is a green house made of?

Glass.

What goes up and does not come down?

Your age.

Tough and Tricky

I only point in one direction, but I guide people around the world. What am I?

A compass.

What has a head and a tail but no legs?

A coin.

What do you call someone who doesn't have all their fingers on one hand?

Normal. You have fingers on both hands.

What was the highest mountain in the world before Mount Everest was discovered?

Mount Everest.

What is higher without a head than with it?

A pillow.

Take off my skin and I won't cry, but you will. What am I?

An onion.

What can you draw without a pencil or paper?

The blinds.

What runs along the street but has no legs?

The curb.

What has holes but still holds water?

A sponge.

What goes up when rain comes down?

An umbrella.

Tough and Tricky

What flies all day but never goes anywhere?

A flag.

What goes around the house and in the house but never touches the house?

The sun.

The more of these you take, the more you leave behind.

Footsteps.

What is brown when you buy it, red when you use it, and black when you throw it away?

Firewood.

Everyone has one and they can't lose it. What is it?

A shadow.

What has many rings but no fingers?

A telephone.

What has two legs but can't walk?

A pair of pants.

What American state is round on both sides and high in the middle?

Ohio.

What kind of ship never sinks?

Friendship.

Why did the bungee jumper take a vacation?

Because he was at the end of his rope.

Why are good intentions like people who faint?

They both need to be carried out.

What is always running but never gets anywhere?

A refrigerator.

When is a door not a door?

When it is ajar.

What's a liquid that won't freeze?

Hot water.

What has two hands, no fingers, stands still, and goes?

A clock.

What gets bigger and bigger the more you take away from it?

A hole.

How can a pocket be empty but still have something in it?

It can have a hole in it.

In a one-story pink house with pink windows, pink walls, pink doors, and pink floors lived a girl with a pink cat which even had pink paws. What color were the stairs?

There were no stairs. It was a one-story house.

A dad and his son had an accident and were taken to different hospitals. Upon seeing the boy, his surgeon said, "I can't operate on you. You're my son." How is that possible?

The surgeon was the boy's mother.

What has no legs but is always walking?

A pair of shoes.

Tough and Tricky

I can breathe and I will eat what you feed me, but if you give me water I will die. What am I?

A fire.

You are lost in a cold dark cave. You have a match, a kerosene lamp, and a candle. Which do you light first?

The match.

A man was driving his truck without his lights on and the moon was not out, yet he still managed to spot a rabbit run out on the road. How?

It was daylight.

If an electric train is traveling south and the wind is blowing north, in which direction would the smoke travel?

There is no smoke from an electric train.

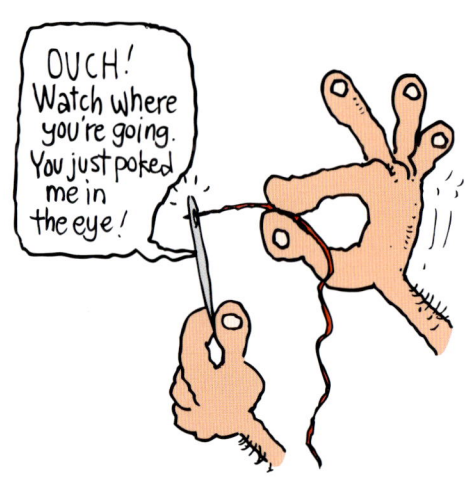

What has an eye but cannot see?

A needle.

What is the only certain way you can double your money?

Look at it in the mirror.

What's the funniest kind of cookie?

A snickerdoodle!

What has a bed but never sleeps, can run but never walks and a bank but no money?

A river.

What loses its head in the morning but gets it back at night?

A pillow.

What has teeth but cannot eat?

A comb.

Tough and Tricky

What sort of person stands around making faces all day?

A watchmaker.

I have keys but no locks. I have space but no room. You can enter but not go inside. What am I?

A keyboard.

What goes around and around the wood but never goes into the wood?

The bark of a tree.

I always tell the truth and I copy everything I see. What am I?

A mirror.

Where do you find roads without cars, forests without trees, and towns without houses?

On a map!

What question can you never honestly answer *"yes"* to?

"Are you asleep?"

Who is your mother's brother's brother-in-law?

Your dad.

Why can't someone living to the north of a river be buried to the south of the river?

Because they are still alive.

What is better than the best thing and worse than the worst thing?

Nothing.

What has no beginning, end, or middle?

A donut.

Tough and Tricky

Tough and Tricky

What's the most boring type of flower?

A daffo-dull!

What do you throw out when you need to use it, and take it back when you don't need it anymore?

An anchor.

Forward I am heavy, backward I am not. What am I?

A ton.

I am lighter than air but even a million men couldn't lift me up. What am I?

A bubble.

What runs across the floor without legs?

Water.

What stays where it is even after it goes off?

An alarm clock.

I have an eye but cannot see, I am strong and fast, but have no limbs. What am I?

A hurricane.

A box without hinges, lock or key, but a golden treasure lies in me. What am I?

An egg.

It's been around for thousands of years but is never more than a month old. What is it?

The moon.

What kind of coat can you put on only when it's wet?

A coat of paint.

Tough and Tricky

What weighs more, a pound of lead or a pound of feathers?

They both weigh the same.

Brothers and sisters I have none, but that man's father is my father's son. Who is that man?

My son.

If you have me you want to share me, but if you share me you haven't got me. What am I?

A secret.

What creature walks on four legs when young, two legs when it grows up, and three legs when it's old?

A person. Babies crawl, adults walk, and elderly people use a cane.

There is a green house that contains a white house that contains a pink house which contains lots of babies. What is it?

A watermelon.

I am mined and then trapped in a wooden case from which I am never released, and yet I am used by lots of people. What am I?

Pencil lead.

What is something you can keep after giving it to someone else?

Your word.

When I tighten it, it walks but when I loosen it, it stops.

A sandal.

You can draw me, shoot me, and load me, but I'm made of nothing. What am I?

A blank.

There are many different types, but the one you pick doesn't do its job. What is it?

A lock.

What is bought in yards and worn by feet?

Carpet.

I'm measured in temperature (degrees) and time (minutes and seconds), but have neither. What am I?

Longitude and latitude.

If a woman is born in China, grows up in Australia, lives in America, and dies in London, what is she?

Dead.

A king, queen, and two twins all lay in a large room. How are there no adults in the room?

They are all beds.

Tongue Twisters

Toy boat (this one looks easy, but say it ten times fast!).

Polly peddled Polish sausage.

Huge imps sink ships, pink chimps use shrinks.

Theoretically, the thirteenth store shouldn't shut.

Neal nearly kneeled nearby.

Tough and Tricky

Harry hurriedly hopped happily.

A big bug bit a bold, bald bear.

Left leg, right leg, red leg, yellow leg.

The poet poetically promised prime political poetry.

Wendy whispered, Yanni yelled, Ryan roared.
Wendy whispered, Yanni yelled, Ryan roared.
Wendy roared, Yanni whispered, Ryan yelled.
Wendy, Yanni, Ryan yelled, whispered, roared.

Sloppy Salina's slippers sadly slipped, sending Salena sliding and slipping.

Mak met Mike; Mike met Mak;
Mike and Mak met Matt;
Mike, Mak and Matt met Mark;
Mike, Mak, Matt and Mark met Bob.

Frieda's frantically funny face froze when the westerly wind wafted.

Wiley Wilma Wilmington was woefully willful.

In general, in January, Jenny generally generalized.

The freezing freezer froze fast.
The fast freezing freezer feels frozen.
The frozen freezer finally defrosted.

Troy Boy bought soy and bok choy with joy.

Black background, brown background, blue background.

Six thick thistles stick.

Barry brought brilliant butter.

Sally's sore sore sure was sore.

You know New York, you need New York, you know you need unique New York.

An imaginary menagerie manager imagined managing many menageries.

Eddie edited it.

Wally wore an Irish wristwatch. When wound, Wally's Irish wristwatch worked well.

"Sure, Samantha," shy Shelley said shyly.
She certainly shook and seemed to shimmy.
Samantha smiled and served shanks.
"Thanks," said Shelley.

Which witch wished which wicked wish?

Unique New York.

Six sharp smart sharks.

She sifted thistles through her thistle sifter.

A box of biscuits, a batch of mixed biscuits.

Peter Piper picked a peck of pickled peppers. If Peter Piper picked a peck of pickled peppers, where's the peck of pickled peppers Peter Piper picked?

She sells seashells by the seashore. The sea shells that she sells are seashore shells I'm sure.

Rubber baby buggy bumpers.

Round the rugged rocks the ragged rascal ran.

A boy stoat stole Troy's toy boat.

Are our oars oak?

Fred fed Ned bread; Ned fed Fred bread.

Girl apes gripe about Greek grapes.

Should Stu choose the shoes he chews?

I slit the sheet and on the slitted sheet I sit.

Is this your sister's sixth sliver, Mister?

A laurel-crowned clown.

The local yokel yodels.

Many an anemone sees an enemy anemone.

Tough and Tricky

Letters and Numbers

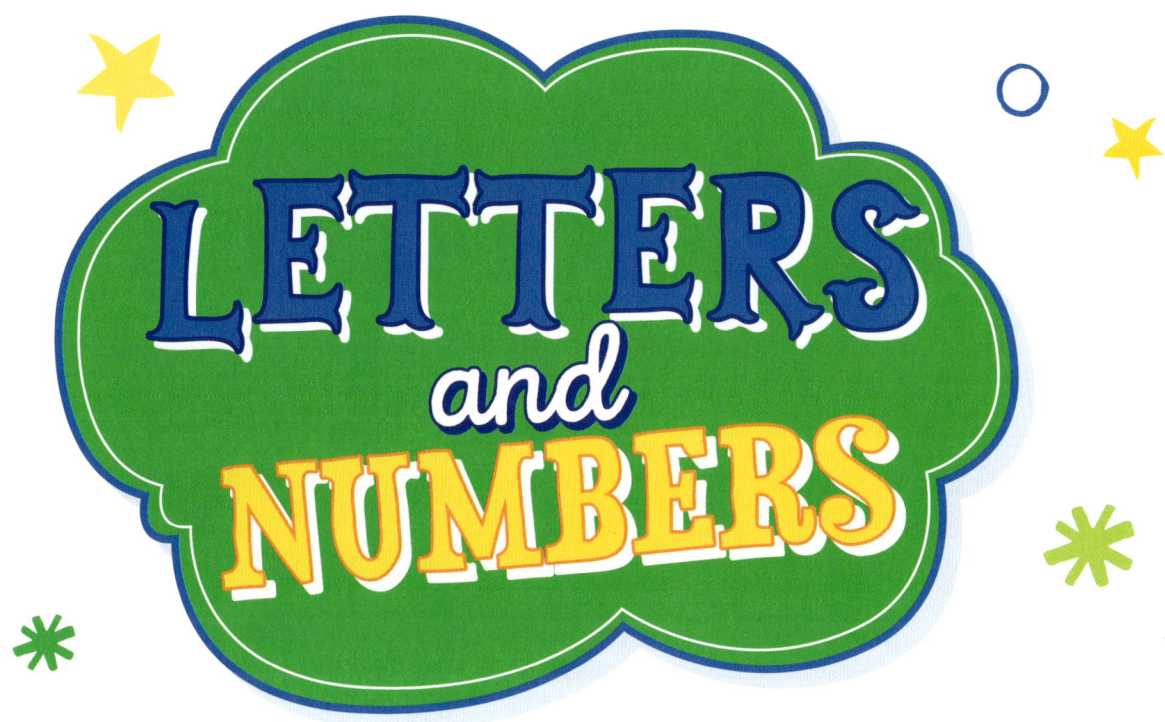

Riddles

What word is always spelled incorrectly?

Incorrectly.

What starts with a "P," ends with an "E," and has a million letters in it?

Post Office.

What ten-letter word starts with fuel?

Automobile.

What is the beginning of eternity, the end of time, and the beginning of every ending?

The letter "E."

When Adam introduced himself to Eve, which three words did he use that read the same backward and forward?

"Madam, I'm Adam."

Two fathers and their sons go fishing. Each catches a fish, which is three in total. How is that possible?

The fishermen are a grandfather, father, and son.

How many 2-cent stamps are in a dozen?

12. There are 12 of anything in a dozen.

What starts with an "E," ends with an "E," and only has one letter in it?

Envelope.

What word if pronounced right is wrong and if pronounced wrong is right?

Wrong.

Letters and Numbers

What has four fingers and a thumb but is not a hand?

A glove.

Which letter of the alphabet holds the most water?

The "C."

Where does Friday come before Wednesday?

In the dictionary.

What's the center of gravity?

The letter "V."

Which months have 28 days?

All of them.

What's the letter that ends everything?

The letter "G."

Name three inventions that have helped man up in the world.

The elevator, the ladder, and the alarm clock.

Why is the Mississippi such an unusual river?

It has four i's and can't even see.

How many seconds are there in a year?

Twelve: 2nd of January, 2nd of February...

When does "B" come after "U?"

When you take some of its honey.

Letters and Numbers

What's green and would kill you if it fell on you?

A pool table.

What is the longest word in the world?

Smiles, because there is a mile between the beginning and the end.

I have ten legs, 20 arms and 54 feet. What am I?

A liar.

Why can't a nose be more than 11 inches long?

If it was any longer it would be a foot.

If Jill has 1.5 sand piles and Jesse has 2.5 sand piles and you combine them, how many sand piles would there be?

One.

How do you get four suits for a couple of dollars?

Buy a deck of cards.

Three men were in a boat. It capsized but only two got their hair wet. Why?

The third man was bald.

What has a hundred legs but can't walk?

Fifty pairs of pants.

What's the hottest letter in the alphabet?

It's "B," because it makes oil boil.

Why was the math book sad?

Because it had so many problems.

When do mathematicians die?

When their number is up.

Two coins add up to 30 cents. One of them is not a nickel. What are they?

A quarter and a nickel. One of them is not a nickel—but the other one is!

When does the alphabet only have 24 letters?

When "U" and "I" aren't there.

Why was the pen going to jail?

He had been sentenced.

I make up all literature, but I'm often sealed. What am I?

Letters.

How do you make seven an even number?

Take off the "S."

Which animals are best at math?

Rabbits, because they're always multiplying.

What word becomes shorter when you add two letters to it?

Short.

What occurs once in a minute, twice in a moment and never in a thousand years?

The letter "M."

What starts with "T," ends with "T" and has "T" in it?

A teapot.

Letters and Numbers

Letters and Numbers

How do you make the number "one" disappear?

Add a "g" and it's "gone."

If two's company and three's a crowd, what are four and five?

Nine.

What has 88 keys but can't open a single door?

A piano.

What do the numbers 11, 69 and 88 have in common?

They all read the same upside-down.

When things go wrong, what can you always count on?

Your fingers.

If you took two apples out of three apples, how many would you have?

The two you took.

What is at the end of the world?

The letter "D."

What did the zero say to the eight?

"I like your belt!"

How did the soccer fan know before the game that the score would be 0-0?

The score is always 0-0 before the game.

What has four legs but cannot walk?

A table.

Why did the cat sit on the computer?

To keep an eye on the mouse.

Fred has five daughters and each daughter has one brother. How many siblings are there?

Six. All five daughters have the same one brother.

What did the robber get when he stole a calendar?

12 months.

How many apples can you put in an empty box?

One. After that it's not empty anymore.

What bet can never be won?

The alphabet.

What has a hundred limbs but cannot walk?

A tree.

What is bigger when it's upside down?

The number 6.

It's flat as a leaf and round as a ring. It has two eyes, but can't see a thing. What is it?

A button!

What was even more useful than the invention of the first telephone?

The second telephone.

Why was number ten scared?

Because seven ate nine.

What is a forum?

One-um plus three-um.

What do teachers and witches have in common?

They both love spelling!

How do you know when a spider is popular?

When it has its own website.

You have a barrel of water and you need exactly one liter of water from it. How can you figure out one liter (L) if you only have a 3L and a 5L container?

Fill the 3L container and pour into the 5L container. Fill the 3L again and fill the 5L from it. There will be one liter left in the 3L container.

The doctor gives you three tablets and tells you to take one every half hour. How long before you run out of tablets?

One hour. You take them at 0 mins, 30 mins and 1 hr.

How can "L" be greater in size than "XL"?

Roman numerals.

How do you share 32 apples evenly with 34 people?

Make applesauce.

What do you call a man who shaves 15 times a day?

A barber.

If you toss a coin ten times and it lands heads-up every time, what are the chances it will land heads-up again the next time you toss it?

50 percent. Every time you toss the coin you have a 50 percent chance of getting heads.

How do you make a witch itch?

Take away the "W."

Tongue Twisters

One smart man felt smart. Two smart men felt smart. Three smart men felt smart. They all felt smart together.

The sixth sitting sheet slitter slit six sheets.

The tenth table tennis championship challenge.

Adam's attempted arithmetic answers were always error-riddled.

Twenty tenors tried tennis.

Sally spelled six synonyms.

Eleven excited elves eagerly exited.

Fourteen fickle fairies failed flying.

Two tooting toucans clap and tap too.

Six hundred and sixty-seven sit-ups sent sick Steve spewing.

Seth said six sick spells. The six sick spells Seth said send Sheldon's silliness soaring. Silly Sheldon shouted sixty-six short spells. The sixty-six short spells Sheldon shouted ensured Seth suddenly ceased saying sick spells.

Sarah's sixth cycling session surely sucked.

The seventh ship sunk the sixth ship.

Sammie spent six Saturdays slouching silently on the sofa.

Crisp crusts crackle and crunch.

Ben sends ten hens to check on six sick sheep.

Eleven lemmings lend Lena eleven lemons.

Ten trumpeters triumphantly trumpeted.

Riddles

When will water stop flowing downhill?

When it reaches the bottom.

Why does the Statue of Liberty stand in New York Harbor?

Because it can't sit down.

What can be swallowed but can also swallow you?

Water.

What do you get if you jump into the Red Sea?

Wet.

Water Works

How does a boat show its affection?

By hugging the shore!

What did the Pacific Ocean say to the Atlantic Ocean?

Nothing, it just waved.

What's another word for tears?

Glumdrops.

What do you call a snowman with a suntan?

A puddle.

How do you saw the sea in half?

With a sea-saw.

What did one raindrop say to the other?

"Two's company, three's a cloud."

What do you get if you cross the Atlantic with the *Titanic*?

About halfway.

Why are rivers lazy?

Because they never get off of their beds.

Why does the ocean roar?

You would too if you had crabs on your bottom.

What goes through water but doesn't get wet?

A ray of light.

Water Works

What do you call a ship that lies on the bottom of the ocean and shakes?

A nervous wreck.

I just knew we should never have gone out in that storm.
And I'm worried about whether the Earth is flat or not.

What happened when the bell fell into the swimming pool?

It got wringing wet.

What washes up on very small beaches?

Microwaves.

What goes in pink and comes out blue?

A swimmer on a cold day.

144

What did the waterfall say to the fountain?

"You're just a little squirt."

What is H_2O4?

Drinking.

Knock-Knock.

Who's there?

Water.

Water who?

Water you doing?

What did the ground say to the rain?

"If this keeps up, I'll be mud."

When a boy falls into the water, what is the first thing he does?

Gets wet.

What is round and deep but could not be filled up by all the water in the world?

A colander.

Why can't it rain for two days in a row?

Because there is a night in between.

Tongue Twisters

Dripping tap, dip your hat.

The big, silver, shiny ship sank.

The stricken sinking sailor signaled S.O.S!

Both blue boats brought bait but the boatmen borrowed Braydon's rods.

I see the sea is shining and the sun shimmers smartly.

Wet Ron wrestled wringing wet Wally wrongly.

Wrinkly Wally really wasted water.

Ruby ran, rode, and read by the wet riverbed.

Ruby waded in the raging white-water river.

Alf frowned as he threw the anchor down.

Bo's brother's boat broke.

Wendy renders Ryan's wall when it's wet and rainy.

A splishy splashy fish was snatched by Mitch.

Funny Flo floundered while Fay found a floaty.

Water Works

Simon swam and Netty snorkled.

Sam swam while Sim swallowed seawater.

Splish, splash, swish, squished fish.

Blake blew blue bubbles in the bath.

Slim Shauna's sure she can swim to shore.

Doug dips, slides, slips, and dives.

Backstroke and breaststroke are both a breeze.

Shimmering Swiss swimmers shimmer.

Sammy sat on a sandy shore and is sure her shorts are sandy.

Steve is a slave to the slow wet waves.

Water sports see Spiro sporting spotty board shorts.

Strange School and Wacky Work

Riddles

Who is the best friend to make at school?

The princi-pal!

What is a math teacher's favorite dessert?

Pi!

What's black when it's clean and white when it's dirty?

A blackboard.

If a butcher is two meters tall and has size eleven feet, what does he weigh?

Meat.

Why was the archaeologist upset?

Because his job was in ruins!

Why do doctors wear masks when operating?

So that if they make a mistake nobody will know who did it.

Why did the teacher keep dialing 9-2 instead of 9-1-1?

Because 1 + 1 = 2!

What did the dentist say to the golfer?

"You've got a hole in one!"

Why couldn't the sailors play cards?

The captain was standing on the deck.

Why are cooks mean?

Because they beat eggs and whip cream!

What's the difference between a jeweler and a jailer?

A jeweler sells watches and a jailer watches cells.

Why can't anyone stay angry with actors?

Because they always make up.

What did the farmer say when he lost his tractor?

"Where's my tractor?"

Why did the boy laugh after his operation?

Because the doctor had him in stitches.

Why didn't the boy work in the wool factory?

Because he was too young to dye.

Why did the farmer plow his field with a steamroller?

He wanted to grow mashed potatoes.

A teacher, a construction worker, and a hat maker were walking down the street. Who had the biggest hat?

The one with the biggest head.

What is the difference between a bus driver and a cold?

One knows the stops, the other stops the nose.

What time do most people go to the dentist?

Tooth-hurty.

What illness do retired pilots get?

Flu.

How did the dentist become a brain surgeon?

His drill slipped.

How did the comedian pass the time in hospital?

By telling sick jokes.

What type of music do geologists like best?

Rock.

How can you tell an undertaker?

By his grave manner.

Why do artists make a lot of money?

Because they can draw their own wages.

How do fisherman make nets?

They make lots of holes and tie them together with string.

What did the dentist want?

The tooth, the whole tooth, and nothing but the tooth.

What's red, white, and brown and travels faster than the speed of sound?

An astronaut's ham and tomato sandwich.

What is a computer's first sign of old age?

It loses its memory.

What do you get when you cross a plumber with a ballerina?

A tap dancer.

Why did the computer sneeze?

It had a virus.

What's the difference between a train station and a teacher?

One minds the train, the other trains the mind.

Why couldn't the boy go straight home from school?

Because he lived around the corner.

What is the easiest way to get a day off school?

Wait until Saturday.

Why was the cross-eyed teacher so frustrated?

Because he couldn't control his pupils.

What trees do fortune tellers look at?

Palms.

I sometimes build bridges of silver and crowns of gold. Who am I?

A dentist.

What's the difference between a cat burglar and a butcher?

One stays awake and the other weighs a steak.

When is homework no longer homework?

When you hand it in to the teacher.

What is a robot's favorite part of the school day?

Assembly.

Why was the computer so tired when it got home?

Because it had a hard drive.

Why do artists never win at sports?

They keep drawing.

Tongue Twisters

The assistant principal's announcement signaled silence.

Steven suddenly stopped serious science study.

Oh my! I'm giving up science and I'm going to start the biggest stamp collection you've ever seen.

Leisel learned lots of lessons at lunchtime.

Suspension, expulsion, detention, yard duty.

Clara took glasses in cases to class. Clara carelessly cracked glasses in classes. Clara's cracked glasses in cases in classes caused chaos.

Aaron, Alex, and Arwin arrived at daycare all alone.

Trudy was tardy attending trigonometry; trigonometry truly was a trial for Trudy.

Leroy liked learning literature.

Peter played politely in the playground at playtime.

Henrietta's horribly hard history homework was hysterical.

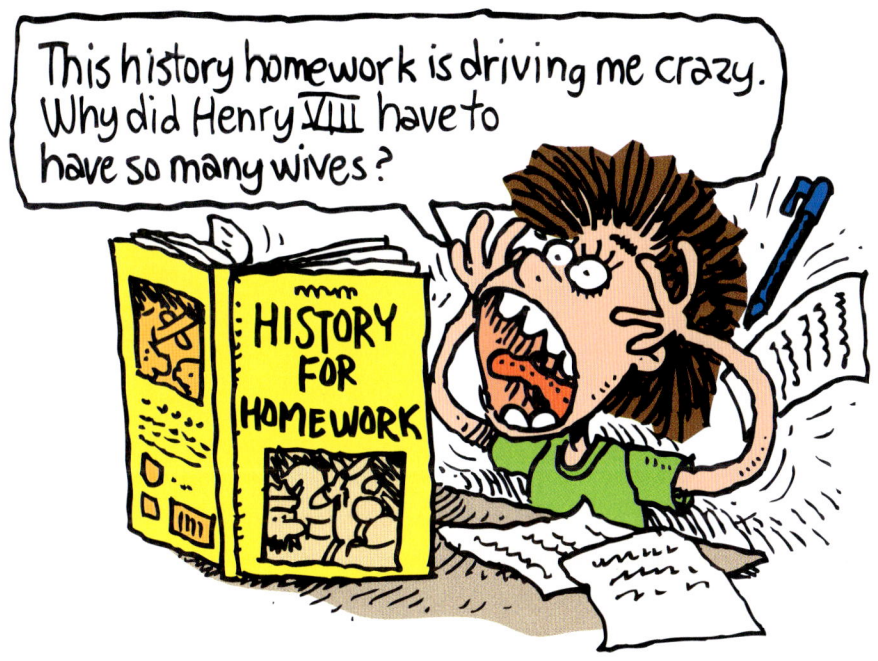

Sirius's sister's slackness ensured slowly slipping science scores.

Frank finally passed physics after frequently failing.

Truant Tracey's truancy tricked teachers.

Geography is generally geographic.

The math course was massively math based.

Cheating Cameron continuously copied Chelsea till checking teacher caught Cameron cheating, causing Cameron to catch a correction.

Elizabeth Hanson studies studiously.

Steven's lunch bag seriously stank.

Sick Steven skipped school.

Teaching trigonometry is tricky.

Danny's detention definitely dragged.

Recess rocks!

Is this a mystical mist myth, Miss?

Salesman Stan's shop stocks short, spotted socks.

Terry told the teacher to try talking tougher.

Detention helped Rita's attention retention.

Polly's shirt shop sold preshrunk silk shirts.

FREAKY FOOD

Riddles

Why don't bananas get lonely?

Because they hang around in bunches.

Lonely? Not likely with this bunch.

How do you make a cream puff?

Chase it around!

What do you get when you cross a baby rabbit with a vegetable?

A bunion.

What are two things you cannot have for breakfast?

Lunch and dinner.

Freaky Food

What kind of room has no door, no windows, no floor and no roof?

A mushroom.

What's the difference between a young lady and a fresh loaf?

One is a well-bred maid and the other is well-made bread.

What has to be broken before you can use it?

An egg.

On what nuts can pictures hang?

Walnuts.

What did one tomato say to the other that was lagging behind?

"Ketchup!"

Which cheese is made backward?

Edam.

Where all the slow tomatoes end up.

Why did the salad practice meditation?

It needed to **ROMAINE** calm.

How do you make a banana split?

Cut it in half.

What kind of cup can't hold water?

A cupcake.

What vegetable goes well with jacket potatoes?

Button mushrooms.

Freaky Food

What did the egg say to the whisk?

"I know when I'm beaten."

What's green, sad, and covered in cinnamon?

Apple grumble.

What do you get if you cross a cowboy with a stew?

Hopalong Casserole.

How do you make a hot dog stand?

Steal its chair.

Who swings through the bakery, yodeling?

Tarzipan.

Why is orange juice so smart?

It concentrates.

Why are teddy bears never hungry?

Because they are always stuffed.

If you have a referee in football, what do you have in bowls?

Cornflakes.

Freaky Food

Did Adam and Eve have a date?

No, they had an apple.

What can you serve but never eat?

A tennis ball.

What's small, white, round, and giggles?

A tickled onion.

When is a door not a door?

When it's ajar!

What type of jam can't you eat?

A traffic jam.

Why do hot dogs have such bad manners?

They spit in the frying pan!

Why do watermelons get married?

Because they can't elope.

Where were potatoes first found?

In the ground.

What is the difference between a hungry person and a greedy person?

One longs to eats and the other eats too long.

What did one potato chip say to the other?

"Shall we go for a dip?"

Freaky Food

Freaky Food

When do you go when red but stop when green?

When eating a watermelon.

Why is milk the fastest thing in the world?

Because it's pasteurized before you see it.

What side of an apple is the left side?

The side that hasn't been eaten.

What happened when there was a fight in the fish and chips shop?

Two fish got battered.

Tongue Twisters

Chop shops stock chops.

A proper copper coffee pot.

The kitchen cutlery clattered and clunked.

The chunky chef got charred cooking.

Samantha slipped on thick, sloppy sauce.

Freaky Food

Corey's cooking class clapped for Cara's crumble.

Practice proper pancake preparation to promise pristinely prepared perfect pancakes.

Greasy, grimy grills gladdened Gareth.

Silly Susan stirred a saucepan of spicy, steaming spinach soup with a spatula.

Arthur halved hairy Harry's hash brown.

Four flattened French fries.

How many cans can Cam cram in a curry?

Fran loved fried flan.

Greg's gluggy gravy got gloopy.

Frank frustratingly flipped forks. Frank's fork finally ferociously flipped.

Swiss watch, Swiss cheese.

Freaky Food

Freaky Food

"*Better bring better butter, Betty!*" Barry bellowed.
Betty bawled, berating Barry for bringing better butter.
"*Bother,*" Betty's brother breathed.

Bunny's bananas burned and Vinny blamed blurry vision.

Sally's silver serving spoon slipped while serving salad.

Betty blew raspberries while Bonny bit blueberries.

Fritz's fired pizza and Percy's fried fish were fresh.

Silly Stuff

Riddles

What has a bottom at the top?

A leg.

What kind of star wears sunglasses?

A movie star.

Why is a ladies' belt like a garbage truck?

Because it goes around and gathers the waist.

What invention allows you to see through walls?

A window.

Silly Stuff

Why did the boy sit on his watch?

He wanted to be on time.

What needs to be answered, but doesn't ask a question?

A telephone.

Where was Solomon's temple?

On his head.

Why did the girl tear a page out of the calendar?

Because she wanted to take a month off.

Why did the boy put his bed in the fireplace?

So he could sleep like a log.

Why do we dress baby girls in pink and baby boys in blue?

Because they can't dress themselves.

What is the longest rope in the world?

Europe.

What is always behind the times?

The back of a watch.

How do you print a pizza?

Use a pizza paper!

What's easy to get into but hard to get out of?

Trouble.

What's the definition of intense?
Where campers sleep.

What is so delicate that saying its name breaks it?
Silence!

Why are false teeth like stars?
They come out at night.

Where can you always find a helping hand?
At the end of your arm.

Why did the belt go to jail?

Because it held up a pair of pants.

What did the stamp say to the envelope?

"Stick with me and we'll go places."

How does a fireplace feel?

Grate!

What's the difference between an oak tree and a tight pair of shoes?

One makes acorns, the other makes corns ache.

What do you get when you cross a frog and a hare?

A bunny ribbit!

What did one wall say to the other wall?

"I'll meet you at the corner."

Can February March?

No, but April May.

When is a chair like a woman's dress?

When it's satin.

What did the tie say to the hat?

"You go on ahead, I'll just hang around."

How long should a person's legs be?

Long enough to reach their feet.

What do hippies do?

They hold your leggies on.

What did the pencil sharpener say to the pencil?

"Stop going in circles and get to the point!"

How do you make a pair of pants last?

Make the coat first.

Can a match *box*?

No, but a tin can.

Why did the traffic light turn red?

You would too if you had to change in the middle of the street!

Silly Stuff

What did the little mountain say to the big mountain?

"Hi, Cliff!"

Where are the Andes?

At the end of your armies.

When is the cheapest time to call friends on the phone?

When they're not home.

What did the big hand of the clock say to the little hand?

"Got a minute?"

What flowers grow under your nose?

Tulips.

What did the key say to the glue?

"Stick with me, I can open doors for you!"

Where does Friday come before Thursday?

In the dictionary!

What sort of star is dangerous?

A shooting star.

Which trees are always sad?

Pine trees.

How do you make fire with two sticks?

Make sure one of them is a match.

What is the only true cure for dandruff?

Baldness!

How many letters are there in the alphabet?

Eleven: T-h-e a-l-p-h-a-b-e-t!

What did the piece of wood say to the drill?

You bore me.

I have every color but no gold, what am I?

A rainbow.

Why did the car get a puncture?

There was a fork in the road.

What dance do hippies hate?

A square dance.

When do clocks die?

When their time's up.

What's green and short and goes camping?

A boy sprout.

What's the easiest way to find a thumbtack you dropped?

Walk around in bare feet.

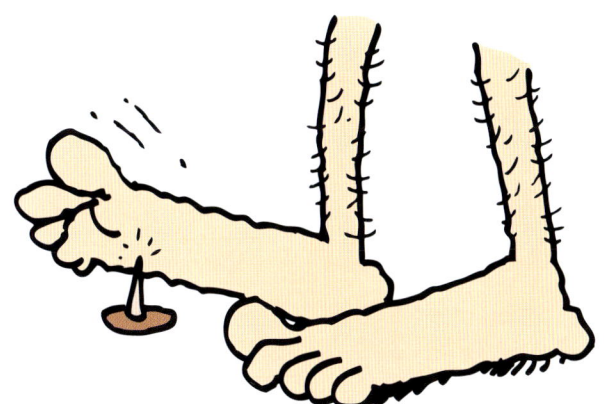

Silly Stuff

What did the big chimney say to the little chimney?

"You're too young to smoke."

What's the easiest way to get on TV?

Sit on it.

Which month has 28 days?

All of them!

Why do you go to bed?

Because the bed will not come to you.

If everyone bought a white car, what would we have?

A white carnation.

Why is a bride always out of luck on her wedding day?

Because she never marries the best man.

Why did the one-armed man cross the road?

He wanted to get to the second-hand shop.

Which organ is the only one to have named itself?

The brain.

You use me from your head to your toes, the more I work the thinner I grow. What am I?

A bar of soap.

Where are English kings and queens crowned?

On the head.

What do you call a lazy toy?

An inaction figure.

How do you catch a squirrel?

Climb into a tree and act like a nut.

Which letter of the alphabet has the most water?

"C."

Why do toadstools grow so close together?

They don't need mushroom.

Why was the broom late?

It overswept.

What are government workers called in Spain?

Seville servants.

Why did the bacteria cross the microscope?

To get to the other slide.

What has a neck but no head?

A bottle.

How often do Christmas Day and New Year's day fall in the same year?

Every year.

What do you call a man with a map on his head?

Miles!

What do you call a man with a shovel?

Doug.

What do you call a man without a shovel?

Douglas!

What do you call a man pouring water into a jug?

Phil.

What do you call a lady in the middle of a tennis court?

Annette.

What five-letter word becomes shorter when you add two letters to it?

"Short!"

What did the left eye say to the right eye?
Between us, something smells!

What do you call a man covered in cat scratches?
Claude.

What do you call a man in a pile of leaves?
Russell.

What do you call a man with rabbits in his pants?
Warren.

What's brown and sticky?
A stick.

What's the coldest country in the world?

Chile.

What kind of song can you sing in the car?

A cartoon.

Why did the girl throw her guitar away?

Because it had a hole in the middle.

Why does lighting shock people?

It doesn't know how to conduct itself.

What can you sit on, sleep on, and brush your hair with?

A chair, a bed, and a hairbrush.

What moves faster, heat or cold?

Heat. Anyone can catch a cold.

How do you use an Egyptian doorbell?

Toot-and-come-in.

What is always the tallest building in a town?

The library. It has a lot of stories.

What word begins and ends with "e" but only has one letter?

Envelope!

Where did the king keep his armies?

Up his sleevies.

Why did the snowman dress up?

Because he was going to the snowball.

If a purple man lives in a purple house and a yellow man lives in a yellow house, who lives in the White House?

The President of the United States of America.

I am red, green, blue, and purple and nobody can reach me—not even a giant. What am I?

A rainbow.

What did the alien say to the gas pump?

"Take me to your leader."

What do all the Smiths in the phone book have in common?

They all have phones.

What turns into a different story?

A spiral staircase.

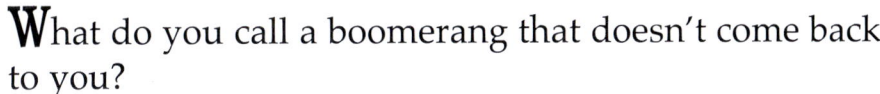

I have all of your knowledge but could fit in your hands. What am I?

Your brain.

What do you call a boomerang that doesn't come back to you?

A stick.

What am I?

A question.

In what month do people sleep the least?
February because it's the shortest month.

Why was the Egyptian girl confused?
Because her daddy was a mummy.

What has a foot but no leg?
A ruler.

Tongue Twisters

Audrey ought to let slight slips go.

Irish wristwatch, Swiss wristwatch.

Ollie's orange organ.

Princess Pauline, the pretty pianist, pluckily played piano.

Silly Stuff

Greg's grimy gooey green glockenspiel.

A particularly pleasant, playful Pop plucked peacocks.

The sliding door silently slammed softly shut.

Peter played pretty perfect ping-pong.

Bobby Buyers bumbled the ball in badminton.

Cameron cruelly cut Christopher's crew cut, causing Christopher to cry.

Patiently practicing picking, plucking, playing guitar.

Faith faces faithfully west. Facing west, Faith faced friends fighting.

Every excellent egg easily excelled at exaggerating.

Bryan's a bald but buffed boxer.

Each Easter, Eddie eats eighty Easter eggs.

The big blue beanbag broke, blasting billions of beans backward.

An accuser alleged Randal's actions as absolutely unacceptable.

Can you can a can as a canner can can a can?

Tiny Tim thought trippy thoughts.

Active Adam asked for answers.

Six short slow shepherds.

Clever Kelly gasps and clasps the glass cask.

Some shun sunshine.

Three free throws.

A truly frugal ruler's mural.

When does the watch shop shut?

Susie sat in a shoeshine shop. Where she shines she sits and where she sits she shines.

Fearful Frankie thought frankly frightening thoughts.

Clean clams crammed in clean cans.

When does Wendy whine about the World Wide Web?

Sure the ship's shipshape, sir.

Wayne really watches walruses in rural Wales.